SCOTT FORESMAN · ADDISON WESLEY

Mathematics

Grade 1

Reteaching Masters/ Workbook

PEARSON

Scott
Foresman

Editorial Offices: Glenview, Illinois • Parsippany, New Jersey • New York, New York

Sales Offices: Needham, Massachusetts • Duluth, Georgia • Glenview, Illinois
Coppell, Texas • Ontario, California • Mesa, Arizona

Overview

Reteaching Masters/Workbook provides additional teaching options for teachers to use with students who have not yet mastered key skills and concepts covered in the student edition. A pictorial model is provided when appropriate, followed by worked-out examples and a few partially worked-out exercises. These exercises match or are similar to the simpler exercises in the student edition.

ISBN 0-328-04965-4

7 8 9 10 V084 09 08

Name _____

Identifying and Extending Patterns

This is a pattern.

  repeats over and over.

This is a pattern, too.

  repeats over and over.

Circle the part that repeats.
Color what comes next.

1.

2.

3.

Name _____

Creating and Translating Patterns

Look at these patterns.

A   B   A   B   A   B

 repeats over and over. AB repeats over and over.

Use pattern blocks. Make a pattern. Draw the pattern.
Then make the same pattern using letters.

1.

A   B   A   B   A   B

2.

S   T

Name _____

Use Data from a Picture

Predict: Will there be more gray tiles
or more white tiles?   more _____ tiles

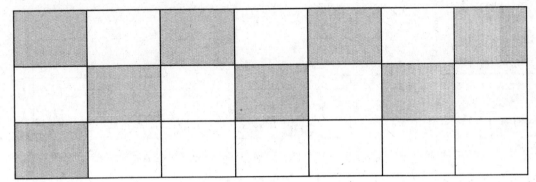

Color the tiles to continue the pattern.

How many gray tiles will there be? __11__

How many white tiles will there be? __10__

I. Predict: Will the belt have
   more gray diamonds or
   white diamonds?   more _____ diamonds

Color the diamonds to continue the pattern.

How many gray diamonds does it have? _____

How many white diamonds does it have? _____

Making 6 and 7

We can show 7 in different ways.

7 is __4__ and __3__. 7 is __5__ and __2__. 7 is __7__ and __0__.

Use counters and Workmat 1 to show 6 and 7.
Draw the counters. Write the numbers.

1.

6 is __2__ and __4__.

6 is _____ and _____.

6 is _____ and _____.

2.

7 is _____ and _____.

7 is _____ and _____.

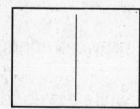

7 is _____ and _____.

Name _____

Making 8 and 9

We can make 9 in different ways.

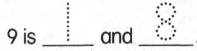

9 is __3__ and __6__ . 9 is __7__ and __2__ . 9 is __1__ and __8__ .

Use counters and Workmat 1 to show 8 and 9.
Draw the counters. Write the numbers.

1.

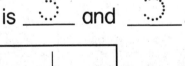

8 is __3__ and __5__ .

8 is _____ and _____ .

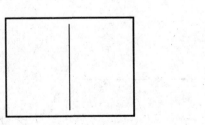

8 is _____ and _____ .

2.

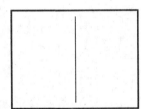

9 is _____ and _____ .

9 is _____ and _____ .

9 is _____ and _____ .

Name _____

Making 10

Here are some different ways to make 10.

10 is 7 and 3.

10 is 4 and 6.

Use counters and Workmat 2 to show 10.
Draw the missing counters. Write the numbers.

1.

10 is ___6___ and ___4___.

2.

10 is _____ and ___5___.

3.

10 is _____ and ___0___.

4.

10 is _____ and _____.

Problem Solving *Number Sense*

5. Make both sides 10. Write the numbers.

10 is _____ and _____.

10 is _____ and _____.

Name _____

Making 11 and 12

We can show 11 in different ways.

11 is __7__ and __4__.   11 is __6__ and __5__.

We can show 12 in different ways.

12 is __8__ and __4__.   12 is __6__ and __6__.

Use counters and Workmat 2 to show 11 and 12.
Draw the missing counters. Write the numbers.

1.

11 is __9__ and __2__.   2. 12 is __9__ and ____.

3.

12 is ____ and ____.   4.

11 is ____ and ____.

PROBLEM-SOLVING STRATEGY

Use Objects

How can Pat put 11 dots on 3 clown hats?

Read and Understand

Pat wants to put all 11 dots
on the clown hats.
She wants to put some dots
on each hat.

Plan and Solve

Use paper for hats. Use counters for dots.
Put some dots on each piece of paper.
Write the numbers to show one of the ways you find.

11 is __4__ and __4__ and __3__.

Look Back and Check

How do you know your answer is correct?

Use counters and pieces of paper.
What other ways can you
put 11 dots on 3 clown hats?

I. 11 is __5__ and __4__ and __2__.   **2.** 11 is ____ and ____ and ____.

Name _____

I and 2 More Than

We can find one more than a number.

Count.	Count.	4 and I more
There are 4.	There are 5.	4 and I more is 5.

We can find two more than a number.

Count.	Count.	4 and 2 more
There are 4.	There are 6.	4 and 2 more is 6.

Use counters to show one and two more.
Write the numbers.

1.

5 and I more is __6__.   5 and 2 more is _____.

2.

9 and I more is _____.   9 and 2 more is _____.

3.

6 and 2 more is _____.   6 and I more is _____.

1 and 2 Fewer Than

We can find one fewer than a number.

Show 6.	Cross out 1.	Now there are 5.

1 fewer than 6 is 5.

We can find two fewer than a number.

Show 4.	Cross out 2.	Now there are 2.

2 fewer than 4 is 2.

Use counters to show one and two fewer.
Cross out counters. Write the numbers.

1.

1 fewer than 7 is ___6___.

2.

2 fewer than 8 is _____.

Problem Solving *Reasoning*

Circle **more than** or **fewer than**.

3.

8 is 1 _____ 9.   more than   fewer than

Comparing Numbers to 5 and to 10

8 is greater than 5.

8 is less than 10.

Use cubes. Circle **less** or **greater**.

1.

    $\dfrac{10}{7}$

    less   (greater)

    10 is _____ than 7.

2. 5

    _____

    less   greater

    5 is _____ than 7.

3. _____

    less   greater

    5 is _____ than 3.

4. _____

    less   greater

    10 is _____ than 8.

Name _____

Comparing and Ordering
Numbers Through 12

We can put numbers in order.

 2 is the least.

 4 is between 2 and 7.

 7 is the greatest.

> The numbers are in order from least to greatest.

Use cubes. Write the numbers in order from least to greatest.

1. 5   3 is the least.

   3   5 is between.

   8   8 is the greatest.

2.   _____ is the least.

   _____ is between.

   _____ is the greatest.

3.   _____ is the least.

   _____ is between.

   _____ is the greatest.

Name _____

It's a Party!

This is a pattern. The balloon and party hat repeat over and over.

Find the pattern. Draw what comes next.

1.   _____

2.   _____

3. How many white balloons are there? _____

4. How many gray balloons are there? _____

5. What color should come next in the pattern? _____

6. If Jeff wants 11 balloons, how many more balloons does he need?

_____ more balloons

Stories About Joining

Join the groups to find how many bugs
there are in all.

Place a counter on each bug. Then count.

2 bugs are on the rock.

3 bugs are on the blanket.

1   2

3   4   5

How many bugs are there in all? _____ bugs

Tell a joining story for each picture.
Use counters to tell how many in all.

1. 2 birds are in a tree.

2 birds are in a nest.

How many birds are there in all? _____ birds

2. 3 fish are in a bowl.

2 fish are in another bowl.

How many fish are there in all? _____ fish

Name _____

Using Counters to Add

R 2-2

Join the parts to make the whole.

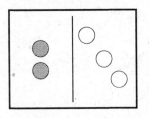

How many black counters? __2__

How many white counters? __3__

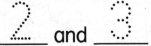 __2__ and __3__ is __5__ in all. 5 is the sum of 2 and 3.

Add to find the sum. Use counters if you like.

I.

How many black counters? __4__

How many white counters? __2__

__4__ and __2__ is __6__ in all. 6 is the sum of 4 and 2.

2.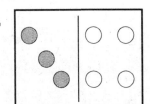

_____ and _____ is _____ in all.

3.

_____ and _____ is _____ in all.

4.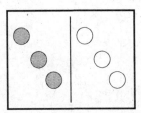

_____ and _____ is _____ in all.

5.

_____ and _____ is _____ in all.

© Pearson Education, Inc. 1

Use with Lesson 2-2. **15**

Name _____

Using Numbers to Add

Find how many in all.

__4__ and	__3__	is	__7__	in all.
__4__ plus	__3__	equals	__7__	.
4 +	3	=	7	

This is an addition sentence.

Tell how many in all.
Then write an addition sentence.

1.

3 plus 1 equals ___4___ .

__3__ __+__ __1__ __=__ __4__

2.

2 plus 3 equals _____ .

____ __+__ ____ __=__ ____

3.

3 plus 4 equals _____ .

____ __+__ ____ __=__ ____

4.

5 plus 2 equals _____ .

____ __+__ ____ __=__ ____

16 Use with Lesson 2-3.

© Pearson Education, Inc. 1

Name _____

Zero in Addition

How many in each part? How many in all?

$3 + 0 = 3$ $0 + 4 = 4$

Write an addition sentence.

1.

$2 + 0 = 2$

2.

___ $+$ 0 $=$ ___

3.

___ $+$ ___ $=$ ___

4.

___ $+$ ___ $=$ ___

5.

___ $+$ ___ $=$ ___

6.

___ $+$ ___ $=$ ___

Name _____

Vertical Addition

There are two ways to show addition.

```
  3
+ 2
───
  5
```

> The sum is the same both ways.

3 + 2 = 5

Add to find the sum.

1.

4 + 3 = __7__

```
  4
+ 3
───
  7
```

2.

2 + 5 = ____

```
  2
+ 5
───
[  ]
```

3.

4 + 2 = ____

```
  4
+ 2
───
[  ]
```

4.

3 + 5 = ____

```
  3
+ 5
───
[  ]
```

© Pearson Education, Inc. 1

18 Use with Lesson 2-5.

PROBLEM-SOLVING STRATEGY

Write a Number Sentence

Write an addition sentence to solve a problem.

2 dogs are sitting.
3 dogs are standing.
How many dogs are there in all?

> ### Read and Understand

You need to find how many dogs there are in all.

> ### Plan and Solve

You can write an addition sentence.

$$2 + 3 = 5$$

> ### Look Back and Check

Does your answer make sense?

Write an addition sentence to answer the question.

1. You have 4 books.
   You get 1 more book.
   How many books do
   you have in all?

   _____ + _____ = _____

---

2. There are 3 frogs.
   4 more frogs come.
   How many frogs are
   there in all?

   _____ + _____ = _____

Stories About Separating

Count to find how many are left.
Use counters to help you.

Jeff has 5 balloons.
2 balloons fly away.
How many balloons
does he have left?

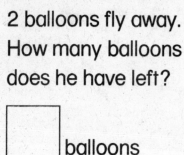
balloons

Use counters to answer each question.

1. There are 6 cars.
2 cars drive away.
How many cars
are left?

cars

2. There are 7 cats.
3 are sleeping.
The rest are playing.
How many cats
are playing?

cats

Using Counters to Subtract

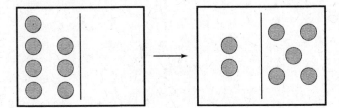

How many counters do we begin with? __7__

How many counters do we take away? __2__

How many are left? __5__

7 take away 2 leaves __5__.

Subtract to find the difference.
Use counters if you like.

1.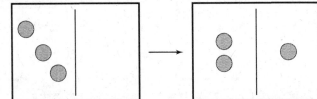

_____ take away _____ leaves _____.

2.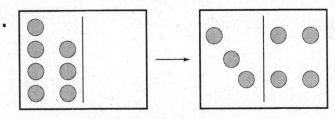

_____ take away _____ leaves _____.

Name _____

Using Numbers to Subtract

Subtract to find how many are left.

This is a subtraction sentence.

__5__	take away	__2__	is	__3__ .
__5__	minus	__2__	equals	__3__ .
5	—	2	=	3

Write a subtraction sentence.

1.

4 minus 1 equals __3__ .

4 — 1 = 3

2.

5 minus 2 equals _____ .

_____ _____ _____

Problem Solving *Writing in Math*

3. Draw a picture that shows subtraction.
Write a subtraction sentence to go with it.

Zero in Subtraction

If you take away all, zero are left.

If you take away zero, all are left.

$$5 - 5 = 0$$ $$5 - 0 = 5$$

Write a subtraction sentence.

1.

   $$4 - 0 = 4$$

2.

   $$3 - 3 = 0$$

3.

   ....
   _____ _____

4.

   ....
   _____ _____

5.

   ....
   _____ _____

6.

   ....
   _____ _____

Vertical Subtraction

There are two ways to show subtraction.

$$6 - 2 = 4$$

$$\begin{array}{r} 6 \\ -\ 2 \\ \hline 4 \end{array}$$

The answer is the same both ways.

Subtract to find the difference.

1.

$$8 - 3 = \underline{5}$$

$$\begin{array}{r} 8 \\ -\ 3 \\ \hline 5 \end{array}$$

2.

$$6 - 1 = \underline{}$$

$$\begin{array}{r} 6 \\ -\ 1 \\ \hline \end{array}$$

Problem Solving *Visual Thinking*

Use the dominoes to fill in the missing numbers.

3.

$$7 - \underline{} = 4$$

4.

$$\underline{} - 7 = 2$$

Name _____

Choose an Operation

Take away 2 flowers.
How many are left?   add   subtract

                                            ⋮3⋮ flowers
                                            ‾‾‾‾‾

Use the picture. Choose **add** or **subtract**.
Write the answer.

1. 6 watermelons are in the garden.   add   subtract
   2 are in the basket.
   How many watermelons are there in all?   _____ watermelons

2. There are 9 carrots.
   2 are picked.
   How many carrots are left   add   subtract
   in the garden?   _____ carrots

3. 5 tomato plants are in one row.   add   subtract
   6 corn plants are in the same row.
   How many plants in all are in the row?   _____ plants

Using Cubes to Compare

Match the white cubes with the gray cubes.
Then count how many more.

How many more
white cubes?   ⋅3⋅ more white cubes

How many fewer
gray cubes?   ⋅3⋅ fewer gray cubes

Write how many white cubes and how many gray cubes.
Then write how many more and how many fewer.

1.

4 white cubes

2 gray cubes

2 more white
cubes

2.

_____ white cubes

_____ gray cubes

_____ more white
cubes

3.

_____ white cubes

_____ gray cubes

_____ fewer gray
cubes

4.

_____ white cubes

_____ gray cubes

_____ fewer gray
cube

Name _____

Using Subtraction to Compare

Write a subtraction sentence to compare.

There are ___2___ more white cubes than gray cubes.

There are ___2___ fewer gray cubes than white cubes.

7 ⊖ 5 ⊜ 2

Write a subtraction sentence.

1. How many more socks than shoes?

____ ◯ ____ ◯ ____   _____ more socks

2. How many fewer hands than mittens?

____ ◯ ____ ◯ ____   _____ fewer hands

© Pearson Education, Inc. 1

Name _____

Bugs, Bugs, Everywhere!

There are 4 ants.
2 more ants join them.
How many ants are
there in all?

> Add to find
> how many in all.

$4 + 2 = 6$

There are 6 ants.
4 ants leave.
How many ants
are left?

> Subtract to find
> how many are left.

$6 - 4 = 2$

Circle the correct number sentence.
Write the answer.

1. There are 5 bees on a flower.
    3 bees fly away.
    How many bees are left?

    $5 + 3 = 8$ $5 - 3 = 2$ There are _____ bees left.

2. 7 bugs sit on a leaf.
    2 bugs join them.
    How many bugs are there in all?

    $7 + 2 = 9$ $7 - 2 = 5$ There are _____ bugs in all.

Counting On 1, 2, or 3

There are 5 cubes in the box.	Add 2 more cubes.		Start with 5.	Count on 2 more.

$$5 \; + \; 2 \; = \; 7$$

1.

Start with __3__. Count on __1__ more.

$$3 + 1 = 4$$

Count on to find the sum.
Use cubes if you like.

2.

$$4 + 3 = \underline{\hphantom{00}}$$

3.

$$4 + 1 = \underline{\hphantom{00}}$$

Name _____

Adding in Any Order

You can add in any order and get the same sum.

$$4 + 2 = 6 \qquad 2 + 4 = 6$$

Add. Write an addition sentence with
the addends in a different order.

1.

$$\underline{5} + \underline{2} = \underline{7} \qquad \underline{2} + \underline{5} = \underline{7}$$

2.

$$\underline{4} + \underline{1} = \underline{} \qquad \underline{} + \underline{} = \underline{}$$

3.

$$\underline{} + \underline{} = \underline{} \qquad \underline{} + \underline{} = \underline{}$$

4.
```
   5
 + 4
─────
```

5.
```
   3
 + 4
─────
```

Name _____

Adding 1, 2, or 3

You start with the greater number when you count on.

5   +   2   = ____

5 is the greater number. Count on.

○○○○○   ⑥ ⑦

5   +   2   = 7

Circle the greater number. Then count on to add.

1.

(5) + 1 = 6

2.

2 + (6) = ____

3.

5 + 3 = ____

4.

3 + 4 = ____

5. 5 + 6 = ____

6. 7 + 4 = ____

7. 1 + 10 = ____

8. 9 + 3 = ____

9. 2 + 8 = ____

10. 7 + 1 = ____

Adding Using a Number Line

To help you count on, circle the number you start at.
Draw to show the addition on the number line.

$$5 + 3 = \underline{8}$$

Add 1, 2, or 3. Use the number line to help you.

1. $4 + 3 = \underline{7}$

2. $2 + 6 = \underline{}$

3. $3 + 6 = \underline{}$

4. $8 + 2 = \underline{}$

5. $\begin{array}{r} 9 \\ +\ 3 \\ \hline \end{array}$

6. $\begin{array}{r} 7 \\ +\ 4 \\ \hline \end{array}$

PROBLEM-SOLVING SKILL

Extra Information

Cross out the information you do not need.
Solve the problem.

> You can underline the sentence that tells what you need to find out.

Dan has 2 dogs.
~~He has one bike.~~
He has 3 cats.
How many pets does Dan have in all?

$\underline{2} + \underline{3} = \underline{5}$ pets

Cross out the information you do not need.
Then write a number sentence to solve the problem.

1. Lin read 3 books last month.
   She read 4 books this month.
   2 of the books were about horses.
   How many books did Lin read in all?

   $\underline{3} + \underline{4} = \underline{7}$ books

2. Tom has 6 model cars. He has 1 model train.
   Tom gets 2 more model cars.
   How many model cars does Tom have altogether?

   _____ + _____ = _____ model cars

3. 1 frog jumps in the water. 2 ducks fly away.
   Then 4 more ducks fly away.
   How many ducks fly away in all?

   _____ + _____ = _____ ducks

Name _____

Doubles

R 3-6

You can use a double to add.

Both addends are the same. They are doubles.

$\underline{2} + \underline{2} = \underline{4}$ $\underline{3} + \underline{3} = \underline{6}$

Write an addition sentence for each double.

1.

$\underline{4} + \underline{4} = \underline{8}$

2.

$\underline{6} + \underline{} = \underline{}$

3.

$\underline{} + \underline{} = \underline{}$

4.

$\underline{} + \underline{} = \underline{}$

5.

How many coins are there in all?

$\underline{} + \underline{} = \underline{}$

6.

How many coins are there in all?

$\underline{} + \underline{} = \underline{}$

34 Use with Lesson 3-6.

© Pearson Education, Inc. 1

Name _____

Doubles Plus 1

We can use doubles to add other numbers.

   2 + 2 and 1 more

$$2 + 2 = 4 \qquad 2 + 3 = 5$$

Find each sum. Use counters if you like.

1.

_____ + _____ = _____   _____ + _5_ = _____

2.

_____ + _____ = _____   _____ + _____ = _____

Write a double or a double plus one for each sum.

3.

Sums of 10

Each ten-frame stands for a group of 10.
You can use a ten-frame to learn sums of 10.

6 ●   4 ○

6 + 4 = 10

6

4

+ ____

10

Fill in the missing numbers to find a sum of 10.
Use ten-frames and counters if you like.

1.

3 + 7 = 10

3
7
+ ____
10

2.

____ + 5 = 10

5
+ ____
10

3.

____ + ____ = 10

+ ____
10

4.

____ + ____ = 10

+ ____
10

---

5. Circle the ten-frame that shows your answer.

Ben has 8 gray counters.
How many white counters does
he need to have 10 counters?

Name _____

Draw a Picture

There are 4 blue buttons.
There are 3 red buttons.
How many buttons are there?

Blue Buttons	Red Buttons

> **Read and Understand**

You need to find how many buttons
there are in all.

> **Plan and Solve**

You can draw a picture of the buttons.
Then you can write a number sentence.
Count the buttons in your picture to find the sum.

$4 + 3 = 7$ buttons

> **Look Back and Check**

How can you be sure your answer is correct?

Draw a picture.
Then write a number sentence.

Bird Stamps   Cat Stamps

1. Dan has 2 bird stamps.
   He gets 4 cat stamps.
   How many stamps are there altogether?

   _____ stamps   _____ + _____ = _____

Name _____

Hop to It!

You can count on to add.

4 rabbits are in the house. 2 more rabbits come.
How many rabbits are there in all?

> Start at 4.
> Count on 5, 6.
> $4 + 2 = 6$.

1.

$5 + 1 = \underline{6}$

2.

$3 + 3 = \underline{}$

3.

$6 + 2 = \underline{}$

---

4. There are 10 rabbits.
2 of them are in the house.
How many rabbits are outside? $2 + \underline{} = 10$

---

5. There are 10 rabbits. 4 of them are outside.
How many rabbits are inside the house? $4 + \underline{} = 10$

Counting Back Using a Number Line

To find 7 − 2,
start at 7. Circle 7.

Now count back 2.

$7 - 2 = \underline{5}$

Count back to subtract.
Show your work on the number line.

1.

$4 - 1 = \underline{3}$

2.

$9 - 2 = \underline{\hspace{1cm}}$

Name _____

Counting Back

R 4-2

You can count back to subtract 1 or 2.

5 − 2 = _____

Start at 5.

Count back 2.

4 , 3
___ , ___

Write the number.

5 − 2 = 3
_____

Count back to subtract.
Use counters if you like.

1.

Count back 2.

3 , ___
___ , ___

4 − 2 = _____

2.

Count back 1.

_____

8 − 1 = _____

3.

Count back 2.

_____ , _____

10 − 2 = _____

Problem Solving *Number Sense*

4. Kit lost 1 crayon.

She only has 9 crayons now.

How many crayons did she start with? _____

© Pearson Education, Inc. 1

0 Use with Lesson 4-2.

Name _____

Using Doubles to Subtract

Doubles help you to subtract.

Think: $3 + 3 = \underline{6}$ so $6 - 3 = \underline{3}$

Add the doubles.
Then use the doubles to help you subtract.

1. $1 + 1 = \underline{2}$ so $2 - 1 = \underline{}$

---

2. $4 + 4 = \underline{}$ so $8 - 4 = \underline{}$

Problem Solving *Visual Thinking*

Complete the addition and subtraction sentences.

3. $2 + 2 = \underline{}$

   $4 - 2 = \underline{}$

PROBLEM-SOLVING STRATEGY   **R 4-4**

Write a Number Sentence

There are 6 birds on the branch.

4 birds fly away.

How many birds are left?

Read and Understand

You need to find how many birds are left.

Plan and Solve

Write a subtraction sentence to find how many birds are left.

$$6 - 4 = 2$$

Look Back and Check

Does your answer make sense?

Write a subtraction sentence to answer each question.

1. There are 8 marbles in the bag.
   3 marbles roll out.
   How many marbles
   are left in the bag?

   _____ _____ _____

2. Mary has 10 pencils.
   She gives 4 pencils to Jack.
   How many pencils does
   Mary have left?

   _____ _____ _____

Name _____

Using Related Facts

$4 + 3 = 7$

$7 - 3 = 4$

> The addition fact and the subtraction fact use the same numbers.

$6 + 4 = \underline{10}$

$\underline{10} - 4 = \underline{6}$

> The sum of the addition sentence is the first number in the subtraction sentence.

Write a related addition and subtraction sentence for each picture.

1.

$\underline{7} + \underline{4} = \underline{11}$

$\underline{11} - \underline{4} = \underline{7}$

2.

$\underline{} + \underline{2} = \underline{}$

$\underline{} - \underline{2} = \underline{}$

3.

$\underline{} + \underline{} = \underline{}$

$\underline{} - \underline{} = \underline{}$

4.

$\underline{} + \underline{} = \underline{}$

$\underline{} - \underline{} = \underline{}$

Fact Families

This is a fact family.

$6 + 3 = 9$ $9 - 3 = 6$

$3 + \underline{6} = 9$ $9 - \underline{6} = 3$

> There are four related facts in this fact family.

This is a fact family, too.

$4 + 4 = \underline{8}$ $8 - 4 = \underline{4}$

> There are two related facts in this fact family.

Write each fact family.

1.

$\underline{3} + \underline{} = \underline{}$ $\underline{} - \underline{3} = \underline{}$

$\underline{} + \underline{3} = \underline{}$ $\underline{} - \underline{} = \underline{3}$

2.

$\underline{} + \underline{} = \underline{}$ $\underline{} - \underline{} = \underline{}$

Using Addition Facts to Subtract

Use addition facts to help you subtract.

6 − 1 = _____

5 + 1 = 6

5 + 1 = 6
and
6 − 1 = 5
are
related facts.

6 − 1 = __5__

Match the addition fact that will help you subtract. Then subtract.

1.

7 − 4 = __3__

5 + 3 = 8

2.

8 − 3 = _____

7 + 2 = 9

3.

6 − 4 = _____

2 + 4 = 6

4.

10 − 6 = _____

3 + 4 = 7

5.

9 − 2 = _____

4 + 6 = 10

Choose an Operation

> Add to find how many in all.
> Subtract to find how many are left.

Marco has 4 pennies.
He gets 2 more pennies.
How many pennies does
he have in all?

(add)   subtract

$4 \oplus 2 = 6$

Maria has 5 pennies.
She gives 3 pennies to Jim.
How many pennies does
Maria have left?

add   (subtract)

$5 \ominus 3 = 2$

Circle add or subtract.

Then write a number sentence.

1. Ruth has 3 coins.
   She gives 1 coin to Bess.
   How many coins does Ruth have left?

   add   subtract

   _____ ◯ _____ = _____

2. Ned has 4 coins.
   He gets 3 more coins.
   How many coins does he have in all?

   add   subtract

   _____ ◯ _____ = _____

Name _____

Playful Puppies

5 puppies play.
3 more puppies play.
How many puppies play in all?

__5__ + __3__ = __8__   __8__ puppies play

Solve. Use related facts to help you.

1. 8 puppies are sleeping and
   3 puppies wake up.
   How many puppies are still sleeping?

   _____ – _____ = _____   _____ puppies are sleeping

2. There are 8 puppies.
   There are 4 toys.
   Each puppy wants a toy.
   How many more toys are needed?

   _____ – _____ = _____   _____ more toys

3. There are 6 puppies.
   4 puppies go outside.
   How many puppies are still inside?

   _____ – _____ = _____   _____ puppies are inside

Identifying Solid Figures

These shapes are solid figures.

| Sphere | Cone | Cylinder | Cube | Rectangular Prism |

Color the spheres red. Color the cones blue.
Color the cylinders green. Color the cubes orange.
Color the rectangular prisms yellow.

1.

Flat Surfaces and Vertices

These solid figures have flat surfaces.

 Cone   Cylinder

These solid figures have all flat surfaces called **faces**.

 Rectangular Prism   Cube

These solid figures have **vertices** or corners.

Use solid figures to complete the table.

Solid Figure	Number of Flat Surfaces	Number of Vertices (Corners)	Number of Faces
I. cube	6	8	6
2. cone			
3. rectangular prism			
4. cylinder			

Name _____

Relating Plane Shapes to Solid Figures

If you trace around the flat surface, you can draw a
flat shape. Draw a line to the shape you would make.

Look at the shape. Then circle the solid figure you
could trace to make the shape.

I.

2.

3.

4.

Identifying Plane Shapes

Plane Shapes

Circle   Square   Triangle   Rectangle

Color the shapes that are the same.

Circle the name.

1.

(square)

triangle

2.

square

circle

3.

square

triangle

4.

rectangle

triangle

Name _____

Properties of Plane Shapes

R 5-5

Count the
straight sides.

A triangle has

 straight sides.

Count the
vertices.

A triangle has

 vertices.

A circle has ____ sides.

A circle has ____ vertices.

A square has ____
straight sides.

A square has ____
vertices.

2.

A rectangle has ____
straight sides.

A rectangle has ____
vertices.

3. Draw a shape with more
than 4 vertices.

4. Draw a shape with more
than 4 straight lines.

Name _____

Same Size and Same Shape

These rectangles are
the same shape.

The rectangles are
the same size.
Count the dots to make sure.

These rectangles are
the same shape.

The rectangles are **not**
the same size.
Count the dots to make sure.

Look at the first shape.
Then color the shape that matches it.

1.

2.

3.

4.

Symmetry

A line of symmetry separates a shape into two matching parts.

These two parts match.

These two parts do not match.

Color the shape that has two matching parts.

I.   2.

3.   4.

Problem Solving *Visual Thinking*

Draw a different line of symmetry on each circle.

5.

Slides, Flips, and Turns

Shapes can slide.	Shapes can flip.	Shapes can turn.

Is it a **slide**, a **flip**, or a **turn**?
Circle the answer.

1.

slide   (flip)   turn

2.

slide   flip   turn

3.

slide   flip   turn

4.

slide   flip   turn

Name _____

Make an Organized List

Give 3 ways you can make this
shape using pattern blocks.

> ### Read and Understand

You need to find all the ways that pattern blocks can make the shape.

> ### Plan and Solve

A list can help you keep track.

Ways to Make ⬯			
Shapes I Used	⬯	△	▱
Way 1	1	0	0
Way 2	0	3	0
Way 3	0	1	1

> ### Look Back and Check

Did you find 3 ways? How do you know?

Give 3 ways you can make this shape using
pattern blocks. Complete the list.

I.

Ways to Make ▱			
Shapes I Used	⬯	▱	△
Way 1	1	0	1
Way 2			
Way 3			

Equal Parts

This apple pie is divided into equal parts.

This apple pie is **not** divided into equal parts.

Each part is the same size.

There are ___4___ equal parts.

Each part is **not** the same size.

There are ___0___ equal parts.

Write the number of equal parts on each shape.

1.

There are ___3___ equal parts.

2.

There are _____ equal parts.

3.

There are _____ equal parts.

4.

There are _____ equal parts.

5.

There are _____ equal parts.

6.

There are _____ equal parts.

Halves

 This rectangle has 2 equal parts.
Each part is one half of the rectangle.
$\frac{1}{2}$ is a fraction that means one half.

Circle the shape that shows halves.
Color one half.

1.

2.

3.

4.

5.

6.

Thirds and Fourths

1 2 3

There are 3 **equal** parts.
Each part is one third, or
$\frac{1}{3}$, of the rectangle.

$\frac{1}{3}$ is shaded.

1 2 3 4

There are 4 **equal** parts.
Each part is one fourth, or
$\frac{1}{4}$, of the rectangle.

$\frac{1}{4}$ is shaded.

1. Circle the shape that
shows one third shaded.

2. Circle the shape that
shows one fourth shaded.

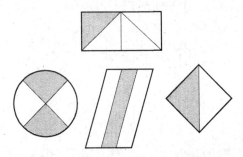

Circle the fraction that shows the shaded part.

3.

$\frac{1}{3}$ $\frac{1}{4}$

4.

$\frac{1}{3}$ $\frac{1}{4}$

Name _____

Fractions of a Set

1 ball is gray.
2 balls in all.
$\frac{1}{2}$ of the balls are gray.

1 ball is gray.
3 balls in all.
$\frac{1}{3}$ of the balls are gray.

1 ball is gray.
4 balls in all.
$\frac{1}{4}$ of the balls are gray.

Tell how many are gray. Tell how many in all. Circle the fraction.

1.

____ hat is gray.

____ hats in all.

$\frac{1}{2}$ $\frac{1}{3}$ $\left(\frac{1}{4}\right)$

2.

____ doll is gray.

____ dolls in all.

$\frac{1}{2}$ $\frac{1}{3}$ $\frac{1}{4}$

3.

____ yo yo is gray.

____ yo yos in all.

$\frac{1}{2}$ $\frac{1}{3}$ $\frac{1}{4}$

Circle the fraction that tells what part of the group is gray.

4.

$\frac{1}{2}$ $\frac{1}{3}$ $\frac{1}{4}$

5.

$\frac{1}{2}$ $\frac{1}{3}$ $\frac{1}{4}$

6.

$\frac{1}{2}$ $\frac{1}{3}$ $\frac{1}{4}$

7.

$\frac{1}{2}$ $\frac{1}{3}$ $\frac{1}{4}$

Non-Unit Fractions

3 parts gray. 4 parts in all.
3 of 4 parts are gray.
$\frac{3}{4}$ of the shape is gray.

3 shapes gray. 4 shapes in all.
3 of 4 shapes are gray.
$\frac{3}{4}$ of the shapes are gray.

Tell how many are gray. Write the fraction.

1.

___2___ of ___3___ cars are gray.

$\frac{2}{3}$ of the cars are gray.

2.

_____ of _____ parts are gray.

$\frac{}{}$ of the shape is gray.

Write the fraction that names the gray part.

3.

4.

5.

6.

Name _____

Use Data from a Chart

How can you give an equal share
of plums to each of 6 children?

The chart shows that there are 6 plums.

Use 6 counters. ○ ○ ○ ○ ○ ○

Fruit		
apples	🍎	12
bananas	🍌	8
oranges	🍊	9
plums	🍑	⑥

	José	Juan	Sol
First give one counter to each child.	○	○	○
Then give one more to each child.	○	○	○

Each child gets ___2___ plums.

Use the chart and counters to solve.
Draw equal shares.

1.

   4 children want bananas.

   Each child gets ___2___ bananas.

2.

   3 children want oranges.

   Each child gets _____ oranges.

Name _____

Shapes All Around Us

Cone   Sphere   Cube   Rectangular Prism

Find the solids in the picture.
Color the cones red. Color the spheres blue.
Color the cubes green. Color the rectangular prisms yellow.

1. How many cubes did you find? __6__

2. How many spheres did you find? _____

3. How many cones did you find? _____

4. How many rectangular prisms did you find? _____

5. Write a number sentence to tell how many
   more cubes there are than spheres.

_____ − _____ = _____ more cube

Minutes

These activities take less than one minute.

These activities take more than one minute.

Does the activity take more or less than a minute?
Circle **more** or **less.**

1.

more   (less)

2.

more   less

3.

more   less

4.

more   less

Understanding the Hour and Minute Hands

The hour hand points to the 6.

hour hand __6__

The minute hand points to the 12.

minute hand __12__

When the minute hand points to 12, say o'clock.

__6__ o'clock

Write the time shown on each clock.

1. hour hand __3__

minute hand __12__

 __3__ o'clock

2. hour hand _____

minute hand _____

_____ o'clock

3. hour hand _____

minute hand _____

_____ o'clock

4. hour hand _____

minute hand _____

_____ o'clock

Problem Solving *Mental Math*

Write the times that come next.

5. 4 o'clock   5 o'clock   _____ o'clock

6. 9 o'clock   10 o'clock   _____ o'clock

Telling and Writing Time to the Hour

Both clocks show 4 o'clock.

4 tells the hour and...

...00 tells the minutes

The clocks show the same time.

Draw lines to match the clocks that show the same time.

1.

2.

3.

4.

Name _____

Telling and Writing Time to the Half Hour

R 6-4

When it is 7:30, the hour hand will be halfway between

_7_ and _8_.

The minute hand

will be on _6_.

The hour hand is shorter than the minute hand.

Complete each sentence.
Then draw the hands on the clock face.

1.

The hour hand will be halfway

between _3_ and _4_.
The minute hand will

be on _6_.

2.

The hour hand will be halfway

between _____ and _____.
The minute hand will

be on _____.

3.

The hour hand will be halfway

between _____ and _____.
The minute hand will

be on _____.

© Pearson Education, Inc. 1

PROBLEM-SOLVING STRATEGY   **R 6-5**
Act It Out

The game starts at 3:00. It lasts 1 hour. When does it end?

| **Read and Understand** |

You need to find what time it will be 1 hour after 3 o'clock.

| **Plan and Solve** |

Show 3 o'clock.   Move the minute hand around the clock one time.   One hour later

___3___ o'clock ⟶ 1 hour ⟶ ___4___ o'clock

Write the ending time. Draw the hands on the clock.

1.

___7___ o'clock ⟶ 1 hour ⟶ _____ o'clock

2.

___11___ o'clock ⟶ 2 hours ⟶ _____ o'clock

Ordering Events

You do things at different times of the day.

<u>morning</u>   <u>afternoon</u>   <u>night</u>

When did each of these things happen?
Write **morning, afternoon,** or **night** on the line.

1.

_____   _____   _____

2.

_____   _____   _____

Estimating Lengths of Time

About how long does each activity take?
You can estimate to find the answer.

(I minute)   I minute   I minute
I hour   (I hour)   I hour
I day   I day   (I day)

About how long does each activity take?
Circle your estimate.

1.

Do homework.

about I minute
(about I hour)
about I day

2.

Wash hands.

about I minute
about I hour
about I day

3.

Build a doghouse.

about I minute
about I hour
about I day

4.

Play a game.

about I minute
about I hour
about I day

Name _____

Use Data from a Schedule

Nature Center Schedule	
Activity	**Time**
Hike	9:00
Feed Turtles	10:00
Pick Flowers	11:00
Bird Watch	12:00

A schedule tells the time at which activities start.

Look for the activity.

The hike starts at _9:00_.

Look at the time.

At 12:00 we _bird watch_.

Use the schedule to answer the questions.
Circle your answer.

1. Which activity comes just before feeding the turtles?

     Bird Watch   Hike   Pick Flowers

2. Which activity comes just after picking flowers?

     Hike   Feed Turtles   Bird Watch

3. What time does the activity, Pick Flowers, begin?

     9:00   10:00   11:00

4. Which activity starts at 10:00?

     Hike   Feed Turtles   Bird Watch

Name _____

Days of the Week

March

1st day	2nd day	3rd day	4th day	5th day	6th day	7th day
Sunday	Monday	Tuesday	Wednesday	Thursday	Friday	Saturday
		1	2	3	4	5
6	7	8	9	10	11	12
13	14	15	16	17	18	19
20	21	22	23	24	25	26
27	28	29	30	31		

There are 7 days in a week.

Use the calendar to answer the questions.

1. Write the days of the week in order.

   Sunday, _Monday_, Tuesday, _____,

   Thursday, _____, _____

2. Color all the Saturdays yellow.   yellow

3. Color all the Mondays blue.   blue

Problem Solving *Visual Thinking*

4. Find the pattern.

   Then write the day of the week that comes next.

   Wednesday, Thursday, _____, Saturday

5. Monday, Tuesday, _____, Thursday

Name _____

Months of the Year

January is the first month of the year.

February is the month **before** March.

March is the third month.

April is the month **after** March.

January
S M T W T F S
1 2 3
4 5 6 7 8 9 10
11 12 13 14 15 16 17
18 19 20 21 22 23 24
25 26 27 28 29 30 31

February
S M T W T F S
1 2 3 4 5 6 7
8 9 10 11 12 13 14
15 16 17 18 19 20 21
22 23 24 25 26 27 28

March
S M T W T F S
1 2 3 4 5 6 7
8 9 10 11 12 13 14
15 16 17 18 19 20 21
22 23 24 25 26 27 28
29 30 31

April
S M T W T F S
1 2 3 4
5 6 7 8 9 10 11
12 13 14 15 16 17 18
19 20 21 22 23 24 25
26 27 28 29 30

May
S M T W T F S
1 2
3 4 5 6 7 8 9
10 11 12 13 14 15 16
17 18 19 20 21 22 23
24/31 25 26 27 28 29 30

June
S M T W T F S
1 2 3 4 5 6
7 8 9 10 11 12 13
14 15 16 17 18 19 20
21 22 23 24 25 26 27
28 29 30

July
S M T W T F S
1 2 3 4
5 6 7 8 9 10 11
12 13 14 15 16 17 18
19 20 21 22 23 24 25
26 27 28 29 30 31

August
S M T W T F S
1
2 3 4 5 6 7 8
9 10 11 12 13 14 15
16 17 18 19 20 21 22
23/30 24/31 25 26 27 28 29

September
S M T W T F S
1 2 3 4 5
6 7 8 9 10 11 12
13 14 15 16 17 18 19
20 21 22 23 24 25 26
27 28 29 30

October
S M T W T F S
1 2 3
4 5 6 7 8 9 10
11 12 13 14 15 16 17
18 19 20 21 22 23 24
25 26 27 28 29 30 31

November
S M T W T F S
1 2 3 4 5 6 7
8 9 10 11 12 13 14
15 16 17 18 19 20 21
22 23 24 25 26 27 28
29 30

December
S M T W T F S
1 2 3 4 5
6 7 8 9 10 11 12
13 14 15 16 17 18 19
20 21 22 23 24 25 26
27 28 29 30 31

Use the calendar to answer the questions.

1. What are the names of the months?

   January, February, _March_, April, May,

   _____, July, August, _____,

   October, November, _____

2. Count the months. How many months are in a year? _____

3. Which month is the first month of the year? _____

4. Which month comes after May? _____

5. Which month comes before September? _____

Name _____

What's Inside the Egg?

1. Jane uses a telescope to look at the birds.

What shape is the telescope?

cylinder

2. At 3 o'clock Jane sees a baby bird.
   Write the time on both clocks.

3. On Monday 1 bird egg hatches.
   The next day 2 bird eggs hatch.
   On what day do the 2 bird eggs hatch? _____

Writing in Math

4. It is April. In 2 months Jane will
   get a pet bird for her birthday.
   In what month is Jane's birthday? _____

Name _____

Numbers to 19

R 7-1

Use counters and Workmat 3.
Write each number as 10 and some left over.

 This shows 10.

 This shows 4 left over.

14 is __10__ and __4__.

1.

17 is __10__ and __7__.

2.

16 is _____ and __6__.

3.

15 is _____ and _____.

4.

18 is _____ and _____.

© Pearson Education, Inc. 1

Counting by 10s to 100

 stands for one group of ten.

10,	20,	30,	40,	50,
ten,	twenty,	thirty,	forty,	fifty,
60,	70,	80,	90,	100,
sixty,	seventy,	eighty,	ninety,	one hundred

$\underline{4}$ groups of ten

$\underline{40}$ forty

Count by 10s. Then write the numbers.

1.

$\underline{5}$ groups of ten

$\underline{fifty}$

2.

_____ groups of ten

_____ _____

3.

_____ _____ _____ _____ _____

_____ groups of ten

_____ _____ _____

_____ _____

Hundred Chart

Use the hundred chart.
Count on from 24.

Start at 24.
Count on by 1s.

24, 25, 26, 27

Count back from 54.

Start at 54.
Count back
by 1s.

54, 53, 52, 51

1	2	3	4	5	6	7	8	9	10
11	12	13	14	15	16	17	18	19	20
21	22	23	24	25	26	27	28	29	30
31	32	33	34	35	36	37	38	39	40
41	42	43	44	45	46	47	48	49	50
51	52	53	54	55	56	57	58	59	60
61	62	63	64	65	66	67	68	69	70
71	72	73	74	75	76	77	78	79	80
81	82	83	84	85	86	87	88	89	90
91	92	93	94	95	96	97	98	99	100

Write the missing numbers. Look for patterns.

1.

41	42			46	47		
51	52		54	55		58	59
		63		66	67		70
		74	75		78		

Use the hundred chart to count back by 1s.

2. 29, 28, 27, 26 _____, _____, 23

3. 31, 30, _____, _____, 27, _____, _____

Counting with Groups of 10 and Leftovers R 7-4

____3____ groups of 10   ____3____ left over   ____33____ in all

Use counters to show the snap cubes.
Make groups of 10.
Then write the numbers.

1. 10 20 21 22 23 24 25 26 27

____2____ groups of ten

____7____ left over

_____ in all

2.

_____ groups of ten

_____ left over

_____ in all

Name _____

Estimating with Groups of 10

Name _____

Name _____

Estimating with Groups of 10

An estimate tells **about** how many.

Circle 10 fish.
About how many more groups
of 10 fish do you see?

There are about   10   (20)   30   fish in all.

Circle a group of 10. Then circle the best estimate
for how many there are in all.

1.

about   10   (30)   50

2.

about   10   20   30

PROBLEM-SOLVING SKILL   **R 7-6**

Use Data from a Graph

This graph shows how many birds are in the park.
How many pigeons are there? Count by 10s.

Birds	
Sparrows	⬚⬚
Pigeons	⬚⬚⬚
Robins	⬚⬚

 is one group of ten.
Count by 10s when there is more than one group.

There are ___3___ groups of 10.

There are ___30___ pigeons.

Use the graph to answer each question.

1. How many sparrows are there?

   There is ___1___ group of 10.

   There are _____ sparrows.

2. Of which kind of bird is there the most?

   _____

3. How many pigeons and robins are there altogether?

   _____

4. How many more pigeons than sparrows are there?

   _____

Skip-Counting Patterns on the Hundred Chart

Skip count by 10s on the hundred chart.

1	2	3	4	5	6	7	8	9	10	⟩ 10
11	12	13	14	15	16	17	18	19	20	20
21	22	23	24	25	26	27	28	29	30	30
31	32	33	34	35	36	37	38	39	40	40
41	42	43	44	45	46	47	48	49	50	50
51	52	53	54	55	56	57	58	59	60	60
61	62	63	64	65	66	67	68	69	70	70
71	72	73	74	75	76	77	78	79	80	80
81	82	83	84	85	86	87	88	89	90	90
91	92	93	94	95	96	97	98	99	100	100

When you skip count by 10s all of the numbers end in 0.

1. Skip count by 5s. Draw a square around the numbers you say.

2. When you skip count by 5s, all of the numbers end in

_____ or _____ .

1	2	3	4	5	6	7	8	9	10
11	12	13	14	15	16	17	18	19	20
21	22	23	24	25	26	27	28	29	30
31	32	33	34	35	36	37	38	39	40
41	42	43	44	45	46	47	48	49	50
51	52	53	54	55	56	57	58	59	60
61	62	63	64	65	66	67	68	69	70
71	72	73	74	75	76	77	78	79	80
81	82	83	84	85	86	87	88	89	90
91	92	93	94	95	96	97	98	99	100

Using Skip Counting

Skip count to find how many.

> Skip count by 2, or add 2 to the last number.

2, ___4___, ___6___, ___8___

add 2   add 2   add 2

There are ___8___ cherries.

1. Skip count by 2s.

2, ___4___, _____, _____, _____, _____

2. Skip count by 5s.

5, ___10___, _____, _____, _____, _____

3. Skip count by 10s.

10, ___20___, _____, _____, _____, _____

Name _____

Look for a Pattern

The children need mittens.

Each child has two hands.

How many mittens are needed for all of the children?

Read and Understand

You need to find how many hands the children have altogether.

Plan and Solve

Make a table to show a pattern. Write the numbers.

Count the children by 1s.

Count the mittens by 2s.

Number of Children	1	2		
Number of Mittens	2	4		

8 mittens will be needed for all of the children.

Look Back and Check

Does your answer make sense?

Find the pattern. Write the numbers.

I. There are 4 boxes.
   Each box has 5 crayons.
   How many crayons are
   there in all?

Number of Boxes	1	2		
Number of Crayons	5			

There are _____ crayons in all.

Name _____

Before, After, and Between

First find 34 on the chart.

1	2	3	4	5	6	7	8	9	10
11	12	13	14	15	16	17	18	19	20
21	22	23	24	25	26	27	28	29	30
31	32	33	34	35	36	37	38	39	40
41	42	43	44	45	46	47	48	49	50

Look to the left of 34 to find the number that comes before it.

33 comes **before** 34.

Look to the right of 34 to find the number that comes after it.

35 comes **after** 34.

34 comes **between** 33 and 35.

Use Workmat 6 if you like.

Write the number that comes before.

1. 23, 24   _____, 47   _____, 19

Write the number that comes after.

2. 32, 33   41, _____   27, _____

Write the number that comes between.

3. 22, _____, 24   45, _____, 47   32, _____, 34

Problem Solving *Reasoning*

Write the number that answers the riddle.

4. I am a number between 10 and 20.

   You say my name when you count by 5s.

   What number am I? _____

84   Use with Lesson 7-10.

© Pearson Education, Inc. 1

Name _____

Odd and Even Numbers

R 7-11

6 is an even number.
It makes equal rows.
There are no extras.

These cubes match.

7 is an odd number.
It does not make equal rows.
There is 1 extra.

These cubes don't match.

Use cubes to show each number.
Try to make equal rows.
Then circle **odd** or **even**.

1.

3

(odd)

even

2.

8

odd

even

3.

9

odd

even

© Pearson Education, Inc. 1

Ordinal Numbers Through Twentieth

Ordinal numbers tell position.

↑ This girl is 1st in line.   ↑ This boy is 6th in line.

Follow the directions to show the position of the flowers.

1. Circle the 1st flower in blue.

2. Circle the 10th flower in red.

3. Cross out the 18th flower.

4. Circle the 12th flower in yellow.

5. Draw a box around the flower that is 15th.

6. Circle the 5th flower in green.

© Pearson Education, Inc. 1

By the Sea

You can skip count to find out how many.

How many toes? Skip count by fives.
Add 5 to each number to get the next number.

5, 10, 15, 20, 25, 30

1. Each boat has 2 sails. If there are 5 boats in all, skip count
   to find how many sails there are.

2, ____, ____, ____, ____

2. Is there an odd or even number of boats?

odd   even

3.

   4th   3rd   2nd   1st

Circle the 1st whale.
Color the 3rd whale blue.

Numbers Made with Tens

You can count the models to find out
how many groups of ten.

2 tens is _20_ .   3 tens is _30_ .   4 tens is _40_ .

Count the models. Write how many. Then write the number.

1.
_1_ ten is _10_

_2_ tens is _20_

_3_ tens is _30_

_3_ tens is _30_ .

2.

____ ten is ____

____ tens is ____

____ tens is ____

____ tens is ____

_4_ tens is ____ .

3.

____ ten is ____

____ tens is ____

____ tens is ____

____ tens is ____

____ tens is ____

____ tens is ____ .

Name _____

Tens and Ones

Here are some ways you can show a number.

Tens	Ones

2 tens 3 ones

Tens	Ones
2	3

2 tens 3 ones   2 tens 3 ones   2 tens 3 ones

23   *23*   *23*

Count the tens and ones. Then write the numbers.

1.

Tens	Ones

Tens	Ones
3	2

_3_ tens _2_ ones   _3_ tens _2_ ones   _32_

_32_   _32_

2.

Tens	Ones

Tens	Ones

____ tens ____ ones   ____ tens ____ ones   ____

____   ____

Modeling Numbers and Expanded Form

The chart shows

Tens	Ones

3 tens   4 ones

3 tens is 30
4 ones is 4
30 + 4 = 34

34 is the same as
3 tens and 4 ones.

Count the tens and ones. Then write the numbers.

1.

Tens	Ones

__2__ tens and __4__ ones

__2__ tens is __20__
__4__ ones is __4__
__20__ + __4__ = __24__

2.

Tens	Ones

_____ tens and _____ ones

_____ tens is _____
_____ ones is _____
_____ + _____ = _____

3.

Tens	Ones

_____ tens and _____ ones

_____ tens is _____
_____ ones is _____
_____ + _____ = _____

Name _____

Ways to Make Numbers

27

_2_ tens _7_ ones

27 = _20_ + _7_

is the same as

27

I ten I7 ones

27 = _10_ + _17_

Use cubes and Workmat 4 to show a different way to make the number. Draw the ones.

1.

32

is the same as

_3_ tens _2_ ones

32 = _30_ + _2_

_2_ tens _12_ ones

32 = _20_ + _12_

2.

is the same as

_____ tens _____ ones

43 = _____ + _____

_____ tens _____ ones

43 = _____ + _____

Name _____

Use Objects

Jo has 11 red balloons and 13 blue balloons.
How many balloons does she have in all?

| Read and Understand |

You need to find how many balloons Jo has in all.

| Plan and Solve |

Make each number with cubes.

Put the cubes together.
Join the tens. Join the ones.

There are __2__ tens and __4__ ones.

Jo has __24__ balloons.

11 and 13

is

20 and 4

| Look Back and Check |

How can you check that your amount is correct?

Use cubes to find how many in all.

I. Dan has 22 books. Mike has 13 books.
   How many books do they have in all?

   There are _____ tens and _____ ones.

   They have _____ books in all.

Name _____

1 More, 1 Less;
10 More, 10 Less

34 take away 10 is 24.

10 less than 34 is 24.

34 and 10 more is 44.

10 more than 34 is 44.

Use cubes. Write the numbers.

1.

23 take away 1 is 22.

1 less than 23 is _____.

23 and 1 more is 24.

1 more than 23 is _____.

2.

1 less than 45 is _____.

1 more than 45 is _____.

3.

10 less than 68 is _____.

10 more than 68 is _____.

Name _____

Comparing Numbers: Greater Than, Less Than, Equal

23 < 33   33 > 23   23 = 23

< means less than   > means greater than   = means equal to

23 is **less than** 33   33 is **greater than** 23   23 is **equal to** 23

Circle **less than**, **greater than**, or **equal to**.

Write <, >, or =.

1.

   (less than)   greater than   equal to

   17 ◯ 24

2.

   less than   greater than   equal to

   45 ◯ 32

3.

   less than   greater than   equal to

   29 ◯ 29

Number-Line Estimation: Numbers to 100

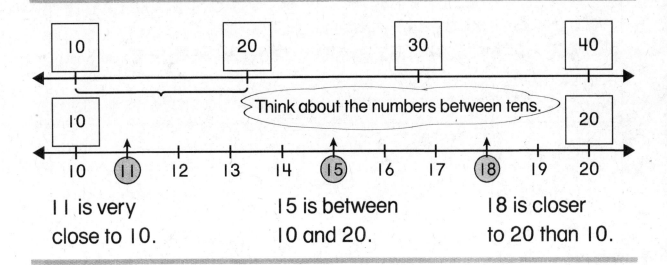

11 is very close to 10.

15 is between 10 and 20.

18 is closer to 20 than 10.

Count by tens to complete the number line.

Then draw lines to show where the numbers go.

1.

2.

3.

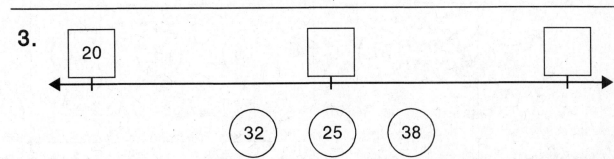

Ordering Three Numbers

The number line can help you put numbers in order.

Show (27) (14) (38) from **least** to **greatest**.

$$\underline{14} < \underline{27} < \underline{38}$$

least   greatest

< means less than
> means greater than

Write the numbers in order from **least** to **greatest**.

1.

60   70   80

(67) (76) (70)

$$\underline{67} < \underline{70} < \underline{76}$$

least   greatest

2.

30   40   50

(53) (43) (34)

$$\underline{} < \underline{} < \underline{}$$

least   greatest

Write the numbers in order from **greatest** to **least**.
Use the number line to help you.

3.

30 40 50 60

(47) (32) (51)

$$\underline{51} > \underline{47} > \underline{32}$$

greatest   least

4.

10   20   30

(16) (6) (26)

$$\underline{} > \underline{} > \underline{}$$

greatest   least

© Pearson Education, Inc. 1

Name _____

Hundreds

Each ▦ stands for 1 hundred.

Hundreds   Tens   Ones

There are 2 hundreds.   There are 3 tens.   There are 4 ones.

__2__ hundreds   __3__ tens   __4__ ones

234

Write how many hundreds, tens, and ones there are.
Then write the number.

1.

__3__ hundreds   __5__ tens   __6__ ones

356

2.

_____ hundreds   _____ tens   _____ ones

_____

Name _____

Sorting

R 8-11

Sort these squares and circles in two different ways.

By Size   By Color

These squares and circles are _big_.

These squares and circles are _small_.

These squares and circles are _gray_.

These squares and circles are _white_.

1. Sort the squares and circles another way.
   Tell the way that you sorted.

These are all _squares_.   These are all _____.

I sorted by _____.

Problem Solving *Reasoning*

2. Circle the shape that does not belong in the group.

© Pearson Education, Inc. 1

Name _____

Making Graphs

Each flower is 1 selection.

Favorite Flower

Count the pictures in the graph.

How many boxes have a daisy? __7__

How many boxes have a tulip? __4__

Which flower is the favorite? __Daisy__

---

1. Ask your classmates to select their favorite drink.
Draw to make a picture graph.

Our Favorite Drink

🍎 Apple Juice									
🥛 Milk									

2. What will you draw to show apple juice? __🍎__

3. What will you draw to show milk? _____

4. How many children selected apple juice? _____

5. Which drink is the least favorite? _____

Name _____

Making Bar Graphs

Each square that is colored gray equals 1 child's selection.

Our Favorite Fairy-Tale Character

Names of Fairy-Tale Characters

Number of selections

Look at the number of squares colored for the princess.

How many squares are colored? __8__

Look at the number of squares colored for the puppet.

How many squares are colored? __6__

Circle the favorite fairy-tale character of the children.

(Princess)   Puppet

---

1. Ask your classmates to select their favorite snack.
   Color to make a bar graph. Then answer the questions.

Yogurt									
Fruit									

   1   2   3   4   5   6   7   8   9

2. Which snack is the favorite? _____

3. How many children selected fruit? _____

Using Tally Marks

The children made tally marks to show the ways
children get to school.

| equals 1

$\bigcirc$ count 5 6 7

卌 equals 5

		Total
Walk	卌 ||	7
School bus	卌 卌	10

$\bigcirc$ count 5   10

---

1. Color some balloons red. Color the rest blue.
   Use tally marks to show how many balloons
   there are in each color. Write the totals.

		Total
Red		
Blue		

Use the tally chart to answer the questions.

2. Of which color are there the most? _____

3. Of which color are there the fewest? _____

4. How many balloons are there altogether? _____

Name _____

Coordinate Grids

This is a map of Felipe's town.
You want to go from the school to Felipe's house.

Read the map. Then complete each sentence.

1. To go from the to the ,

   go __1__ block right and __2__ blocks up.

2. To go from the to the ,

   go _____ block left and _____ block up.

3. To go from the to the ,

   go _____ blocks left and _____ block up.

Name _____

Use Data from a Map

This is a map of a neighborhood.

How many blocks is it from the house to the park?

Step 1:

You need to find out how many blocks in all.

Step 2:

Look at the map.

Find the house.

Find the park.

From house to store ___3___ blocks.

From store to park ___2___ blocks.

Step 3:

Write an addition sentence.

___3___ + ___2___ = ___5___ blocks

It is 5 blocks from the house to the park.

---

1. How many blocks is it from the park to the school?
   Find the shortest path. Write an addition sentence.

   From the 🌳🌳 to the 🏛 _____ blocks

   From the 🏛 to the 🏫 _____ blocks

   _____ + _____ = _____ blocks

Name _____

Let's Make Soup!

Count the striped fish. Make 1 tally mark for each striped fish. Count the dotted fish. Make 1 tally mark for each dotted fish. Write the totals.

> Remember
> 卌 equals 5.

		Total
striped fish	卌 |||	
dotted fish	卌 ||	

Look back and check.

Count the striped fish again. How many are there? __8__
Count the tally marks for striped fish.

What is the total? __8__

Are the numbers the same? __yes__

1. How many dotted fish did you count? _____

2. How many dotted fish are on the tally chart? _____

3. How many fewer dotted fish are there than striped fish? _____

4. Circle the picture that shows what you wrote on the tally chart.

 <   >

Nickel and Penny

> A nickel = 5 cents.
> Skip count by 5s for nickels.

> A penny = I cent
> Count by I s for pennies.

> Skip count by 5s for the nickels.
> Then count on by I s for the pennies.

						In All
5¢ →	10¢ →	15¢ →	16¢ →	17¢ →	18¢	18¢

Skip count by 5s and count on by I s to find
how much money in all.

I.

						In All
5¢	10¢	11¢	___¢	___¢	___¢	___¢

2.

						In All
___¢	___¢	___¢	___¢	___¢	___¢	___¢

Name _____

A dime = 10 cents.
Skip count by 10s for dimes.

A penny = 1 cent.
Count by 1s for pennies.

Skip count by 10s. Then count on by 1s.

10¢ → 20¢ → 30¢ → 40¢ → 41¢ → 42¢

In All
42¢

Skip count by 10s and count on by 1s to find
how much money in all.

1.

10¢ 20¢ 30¢ ____¢ ____¢ ____¢

In All
____¢

2.

____¢ ____¢ ____¢ ____¢ ____¢ ____¢

In All
____¢

Counting Dimes and Nickels

Count dimes by 10s.   Count nickels by 5s.

Count the dimes first.   Then count the nickels.

					In All
10 ¢ →	20 ¢ →	25 ¢ →	30 ¢ →	35 ¢	35 ¢

Count on. Then write how much money in all.

1.

10 ¢   15 ¢ ____ ¢ ____ ¢ ____ ¢

In All
____ ¢

2.

____ ¢ ____ ¢ ____ ¢ ____ ¢ ____ ¢ ____ ¢

In All
____ ¢

Counting Dimes, Nickels, and Pennies

When you count coins, start with the coin that is worth the most.

A dime is worth more than a nickel.
A nickel is worth more than a penny.

Count dimes by 10s.   Count nickels by 5s.   Count pennies by 1s.

10¢ → 20¢ → 30¢ → 35¢ → 40¢ → 41¢   In All 41¢

Count on. Then write how much money in all.

1.

10¢ 20¢ 25¢ ____¢ ____¢ ____¢   In All ____¢

2.

____¢ ____¢ ____¢ ____¢ ____¢ ____¢   In All ____¢

Name _____

Use Data from a Table

Meg buys a top.
She gives the clerk a dime.
Will she get change?

Toys		
Top	🌀	9¢
Ball	⚫	7¢
Jacks	✻✻✻	5¢

The price of the toy is on the same line as the toy.

Find the top in the table.
How much is a top?

A top is __9__ ¢.

Read the story again.
How much money did Meg give the clerk?

Meg gave the clerk __a dime__.

A dime is 10¢.

10¢ is more than 9¢.

Will Meg get change? __yes__

Use the table above. Circle **yes** or **no**.

	You Buy	You Use	Will you get change?
I.	(ball)	(nickel) (penny) (penny)	yes no
2.	(jacks)	(dime)	yes no

© Pearson Education, Inc. 1

Name _____

Quarter

There are different ways you can make 25 cents.

Skip count by 10s
and then by 5s.

$\underset{\textrm{¢}}{10} \rightarrow \underset{\textrm{¢}}{20} \rightarrow \underset{\textrm{¢}}{25} \quad \underset{\textrm{¢}}{10} \rightarrow \underset{\textrm{¢}}{15} \rightarrow \underset{\textrm{¢}}{20} \rightarrow \underset{\textrm{¢}}{25}$

Count each group of coins.

Circle the group of coins in each row that equals 25 cents.

1.

2.

3.

Problem Solving *Visual Thinking*

4. Chris has 4 coins in her purse.
   They are worth 25¢ in all.
   Draw the other 2 coins.

Name _____

Counting Sets of Coins

 > > >   Remember > stands for greater than.

Count the coins. Start with the coin that is worth the most money.

Count on by 10s.   Count on by 5s.   Count on by 1s.

25¢ → 35¢ → 45¢ → 50¢ → 55¢ → 56¢ → 57¢.

In All
57¢

Count on. Then write how much money in all.

1.

25¢ 35¢ ____¢ ____¢ ____¢ ____¢

In All
____¢

2.

____¢ ____¢ ____¢ ____¢ ____¢ ____¢

In All
____¢

Name _____

Half-Dollar and Dollar

Here are some ways to show one dollar.

dollar bill	dollar coin
	or
$1.00 = 100¢	$1.00 = 100¢

half-dollar coin

 or

half-dollar = 50¢
2 half-dollars = 100¢

4 quarters

25¢ → 50¢ → 75¢ → 100¢

4 quarters = 100¢

Circle the group of coins in each row that makes $1.00.

1.

2.

3.

© Pearson Education, Inc. 1

Use with Lesson 9-8.

Name _____

PROBLEM-SOLVING STRATEGY   R 9-9

Try, Check, and Revise

Jim bought 2 toys at the toy fair. Together they cost 11¢.
Which toys did he buy?

Read and Understand

Pick two toys. Find their total.

Plan and Solve

Try 🚗 and 🔍.

Add. __6__¢ + __8__¢ = __14__¢

$\boxed{14¢ \text{ is more than } 11¢.}$

Find a toy that costs less than 🔍.

The ⚾ costs less.

Try the 🚗 and ⚾.

Add. __6__¢ + __5__¢ = __11__¢

Jim bought the 🚗 and ⚾.

Look Back and Check

How can you check your answer?

I. Circle the 2 toys that cost 15¢.

_____¢ + _____¢ = _____¢

What Can You Buy?

Circle the coins you need to buy 1 bear.

Check your answer.

How much is the bear? ____8____ ¢

Count the coins you circled.

How much are they worth? ____8____ ¢

Do the coins equal the price of the bear? ____yes____

1. Circle the coins you need to buy 2 bears.

_____

2. Is the price of the 2 bears
   an odd or even number?   _____

_____

3. Circle the coins you need to buy the puzzle.

Name _____

Estimating, Measuring, and Comparing Length

Look at the paper clip.

Look at the string.

Estimate: How many paper clips long is the string?

About __5__ paper clips long.

Now measure.

> Line up the first paper clip with the edge.

> Be sure paper clips are all the same size.

> Be sure you put the paper clips right next to each other.

Measure: About __6__ paper clips long.

That is close to the estimate.

Estimate. Then measure using paper clips.

	Estimate.	Measure.
1.	about _____ ⌐	_____ ⌐
2.	about _____ ⌐	_____ ⌐
3.	about _____ ⌐	_____ ⌐

Name _____

Use Logical Reasoning

Predict: Will you need more chalk or
more paper clips to measure the marker?

more or more

Read and Understand

You must find out if you need more chalk or more paper clips.

Plan and Solve

Use reasoning to help you.
The paper clip is shorter.
You will probably need more paper clips.

more   more   Measure to check.

Look Back and Check

Measure to check your prediction.
Was your prediction correct?

about __8__

about __5__

Will it take fewer pieces of chalk or fewer paper clips?
Circle your prediction. Then measure.

Measure to check.

I.

fewer

fewer

about _____

about _____

© Pearson Education, Inc. 1

Name _____

Estimating and Measuring with Inches

This is 1 inch. [ruler showing 1 inch]

About how
many inches
long is this ribbon?

About __6__ inches long.
Measure. Use a ruler.

Line up the edge
of the ribbon
with the edge of
the ruler.

The ribbon measures __5__ inches long.
Was your estimate correct?

Estimate the length. Then measure using a ruler.

1.

Estimate.

about _____ inches

Measure.

_____ inches

Name _____

Estimating and Measuring with Feet

A foot is 12 inches long.
This football is about 1 foot long.
An inch ruler is 1 foot long.

About how long is your desk?

about _____ feet long

You can use an inch ruler to measure the length of your desk.

Mark the place where your ruler ends.
Then start measuring again at that mark.

I foot   I foot

The desk measures about __2__ feet long.
Was your estimate close?

Find each object in your classroom.
Estimate. Then measure the length using a ruler.

1.

Estimate. about _____ feet long

Measure. about _____ feet long

2.

Estimate. about _____ feet long

Measure. about _____ feet long

Name _____

Estimating and Measuring with Centimeters

This is 1 centimeter high.

About how many centimeters high is this eraser?

The eraser is about __2__ centimeters high.
Use a centimeter ruler to measure the eraser.

When you measure height, you measure up and down.

The eraser measures __3__ centimeters.
The estimate is close.

Estimate the height. Then measure using a centimeter ruler.

1.
Estimate.

about _____
centimeters

Measure.

about _____
centimeters

2.
Estimate.

about _____
centimeters

Measure.

about _____
centimeters

3.
Estimate.

about _____
centimeters

Measure.

about _____
centimeters

4.
Estimate.

about _____
centimeters

Measure.

about _____
centimeters

Understanding Perimeter

Count the inches around a shape to find the perimeter.

The perimeter of the shape is __12__ inches.

How many inches around each shape?

1.

The perimeter
of the triangle is _____ inches.

2.

The perimeter
of the shape is _____ inches.

Look Back and Check

How many triangle pattern blocks will cover this shape?
Check your answers to be sure they make sense.

Mai says 4 triangle
pattern blocks will
cover this shape.

Does her answer make sense?

Check. Put triangle blocks
over the shape.

Circle the answer that makes sense.

4 pattern blocks   (6 pattern blocks)

How many triangle pattern blocks will cover each shape?
Circle the answer that makes sense.

I.

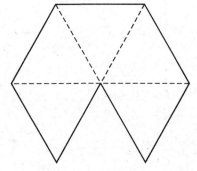

(5 pattern blocks)

8 pattern blocks

2.

10 pattern blocks

14 pattern blocks

Estimating, Measuring, and Comparing Capacity

This holds 1 cup of rice.

This object holds about 2 cups of rice.

About how many cups of rice will this object hold?

Estimate.

About how many cups of rice will fill this object?

Think: How many cups will it hold.

about __5__ cups

Measure.

How many cups of rice will fill the object?

Fill it with rice to measure.

about __6__ cups

Estimate how many cups of rice will fill **each** object.
Circle your estimate. Then measure.

1.

   Estimate.
   about 4 cups

   (about 12 cups)

   Measure. about _____ cups

2.

   Estimate.
   about 3 cups

   about 7 cups

   Measure. about _____ cups

Problem Solving *Estimation*

3. Circle the container that holds about 5 cups.

Name _____

Cups, Pints, and Quarts

Remember: < stands for less than.

Estimate. How much milk will fill the pitcher?

about I

about I

Circle the best estimate.

1.

about I

about I

2.

about I

about I

3.

more than I

less than I

4.

more than I

less than I

© Pearson Education, Inc. 1

Liters

Estimate how much each real object will hold when filled.

> A small container holds a little.

> A large container holds a lot.

Less than a liter	About a liter	More than a liter

Draw a line to the best estimate.

1.

less than 1 liter

more than 1 liter

---

2.   less than 1 liter

   more than 1 liter

3.   less than 1 liter

   more than 1 liter

Estimating, Measuring, and Comparing Weight

Does not balance.	Balances.	Does not balance.
The orange is heavier than 2 cubes.	9 cubes are as heavy as the orange.	20 cubes are heavier than the orange.

Estimate how many cubes it will take to balance.
Then measure.

1.

Estimate.

about _____ 🔲

Measure.

about _____ 🔲

2.

Estimate.

about _____ 🔲

Measure.

about _____ 🔲

3.

Estimate.

about _____ 🔲

Measure.

about _____ 🔲

4.

Estimate.

about _____ 🔲

Measure.

about _____ 🔲

Name _____

Pounds

This weight is 1 pound.

The light bulb weighs less than 1 pound.

The melon weighs about 1 pound.

The dog weighs more than 1 pound.

Circle the best estimate.

1.

less than 1 pound	more than 1 pound

2.

less than 1 pound	more than 1 pound

3.

less than 1 pound	more than 1 pound

Name _____

Grams and Kilograms

This feather measures about 1 gram.
1 gram is lighter than 1 kilogram.

This book measures about 1 kilogram.
1 kilogram is heavier than 1 gram.

Circle the best estimate.

1.   about 1 gram   about 1 kilogram

2.   about 1 gram   about 1 kilogram

3.   about 1 gram   about 1 kilogram

Measuring Temperature

The colored part of a thermometer
measures the temperature.
It tells how hot or how cold it is.

Not much of the colored
part means cold.

A lot of the colored
part means hot.

Circle the thermometer that shows the temperature.

I.

°F 75   °F 20

2.

°C 34   °C 2

3.

°F 90   °F 10

4.

°C 40   °C 0

Name _____

Choosing a Measurement Tool

R 10-15

A thermometer measures how hot or cold it is.

A ruler measures how long or how tall an object is.

A scale measures how heavy an object is.

A measuring cup measures how much something can hold.

Circle the best tool to use for the measurement.

1. How heavy is it?

2. How long is it?

3. How hot is it?

4. How much will it hold?

© Pearson Education, Inc. 1

Use with Lesson 10-15. **129**

Certain or Impossible

This spinner has only 3s on it.

This spinner has no 3s on it.

I am certain to land on a 3.

It is impossible for me to land on 3.

Are you certain to land on 4 or is it impossible?

I.

certain

(impossible)

2.

certain

impossible

Are you certain to land on black or is it impossible?

3.

certain

impossible

4.

certain

impossible

Color the cubes so that the sentence is true.

5. It is impossible to pick a red cube.

Name _____

More Likely or Less Likely

There are more gray cubes in the bag than there are white cubes.

Pick a cube. 🔲
Make a tally mark.
Put the cube back
in the bag. Pick
another cube. 🔲
Make a tally mark.
Put the cube back
in the bag.

Color	Tally
Gray	||
White	

Since there are more gray cubes in the bag, it is more likely you will pick gray.

Fill a bag with 10 blue and 3 red cubes.
Pick a cube. Mark a tally for your pick.
Put the cube back. Do this 10 times.
Mark a tally for each pick.

1.

Color	Tally
Blue	
Red	

2. **Predict:** Which color cube is it more likely you will pick next?

_____

Name _____

Stir-Fry It!

Japanese chopsticks are shorter than Chinese
chopsticks. Japanese chopsticks are about 8 inches
long. Is 8 inches more than 2 centimeters or less
than 2 centimeters?

more than 2 centimeters

Check your answer.
Use your centimeter ruler to show
2 centimeters. Use your inch ruler
to show 8 inches.

Does your answer make sense?

> I don't need to show all 8 inches.
> 2 inches is longer than 2 centimeters.

---

1. Jerry wants to make a pair of chopsticks.
   The chopsticks will be 8 inches long.
   The wood Jerry will use is 1 foot long.
   Is 8 inches more than a foot or less than a foot?

   _____

2. The wood cost 35¢. Jerry gave the clerk
   a quarter and 2 nickels. Did he get change? _____

Writing in Math

3. Ask the children in your class if they have ever eaten
   with chopsticks. Make a tally chart to show their answers.

Doubles

When you add the same number to itself, you are using doubles.

◇   1
◇ + 1
   2

◇◇   2
◇◇ + 2
   4

◇◇◇   3
◇◇◇ + 3
   6

◇◇◇◇   4
◇◇◇◇ + 4
   8

Use doubles to add. Draw doubles to help you.

1. ◇◇◇◇◇   5
◇◇◇◇◇ + 5
   10

2. ○○○○○○   6
   + 6

3. ○○○○○○○   7
   + 7

4. ○○○○○○○○   8
   + 8

Problem Solving *Visual Thinking*

5. For each picture write an addition sentence
   that tells how many buttons there are.

___2___ + _____ = _____   _____ + _____ = _____

Name _____

Doubles Plus I and Doubles Minus I

You can use a doubles fact to help you add one more
or one less.

		Add I more to 4 + 4.		Take I away from 4 + 4.

```
   4                    4                    4
 + 4                  + 5                  + 3
 ───                  ───                  ───
   8                    9                    7
```

Add I more or take I away from each doubles fact.

1.
```
   3                    3                    3
 + 3                  + 4                  + 2
 ───                  ───                  ───
   6                    7                    5
```

2.
```
   5                    5                    5
 + 5                  + 6                  + 4
 ───                  ───                  ───
```

3.
```
   6                    6                    6
 + 6                  + 7                  + 5
 ───                  ───                  ───
```

Problem Solving *Mental Math*

Answer each question.

4. Don has 8 red balloons.
   He has 9 yellow balloons.
   How many balloons does
   Don have in all?

   _____ balloons

5. Kit has 5 blue balloons.
   She has 4 orange balloons.
   How many balloons does
   Kit have in all?

   _____ balloons

Name _____

Adding 10

You can use tens to add.

This is one group of 10.   This is 10 and 1 more.   This is 10 and 3 more.

10          $10 + 1 = 11$ $10 + 3 = 13$

Draw counters. Then find the sum.

1.

$10 + 5 = \underline{15}$

2.

$10 + 6 = \underline{}$

3.

$10 + 7 = \underline{}$

4.

$10 + 4 = \underline{}$

5.

$10 + 9 = \underline{}$

6.

$10 + 8 = \underline{}$

Making 10 to Add

Making 10 can help you add.

Add 7 + 4.   Make a 10.

  →   →

So 7 + 4 and 10 + 1 have the same sum.

$$7 + 4 = \underline{11} \text{ and } 10 + 1 = \underline{11}$$

Use counters and Workmat 2.
Draw the counters. Then write the sums.

1.

$$\begin{array}{r} 8 \\ + 5 \\ \hline 13 \end{array}$$

$$\begin{array}{r} 10 \\ + 3 \\ \hline 13 \end{array}$$

2.

$$\begin{array}{r} 9 \\ + 6 \\ \hline \end{array}$$

$$\begin{array}{r} 10 \\ + 5 \\ \hline \end{array}$$

3.

$$\begin{array}{r} 7 \\ + 6 \\ \hline \end{array}$$

$$\begin{array}{r} 10 \\ + 3 \\ \hline \end{array}$$

Applying Addition Fact Strategies

$$\begin{array}{r} 6 \\ + 5 \\ \hline \end{array}$$

6 + 5 is close to 6 + 6. I can use doubles minus 1 to add.

$$\begin{array}{r} 6 \\ + 6 \\ \hline 12 \end{array}$$

$$\begin{array}{r} 6 \\ + 5 \\ \hline 11 \end{array}$$

$$\begin{array}{r} 9 \\ + 5 \\ \hline \end{array}$$

9 is close to 10. I can make a 10.

$$\begin{array}{r} 9 \\ + 5 \\ \hline 14 \end{array}$$

$$\begin{array}{r} 10 \\ + 4 \\ \hline 14 \end{array}$$

Add. Then circle the strategy you used.

1.
$$\begin{array}{r} 8 \\ + 3 \\ \hline \end{array}$$

doubles

(make a ten)

Think: 8 is close to 10.

2.
$$\begin{array}{r} 5 \\ + 4 \\ \hline \end{array}$$

doubles

make a ten

Think: 5 + 4 is close to 5 + 5. I can use doubles minus 1 to add.

3.
$$\begin{array}{r} 7 \\ + 5 \\ \hline \end{array}$$

doubles

make a ten

Think: 7 is close to 10. I can make a ten.

Adding Three Numbers

When you add three numbers, look for facts you know.
Then add the other number.

⑥
④ 6 + 4 = 10

+ 3   10 + 3 = 13
———
13

The numbers
are in a
different order.

4
③ 3 + 6 = 9

+⑥ 9 + 4 = 13
———
13

The sum is the same.

Find each sum. Add the circled numbers first.
Then add the other number.

1.
⑤
2   5 + 5 = __10__
+⑤
———
12   __10__ + 2 = __12__

5
② 2 + 5 = __7__
+⑤
———
12   __7__ + 5 = __12__

2.
③
⑥ 3 + 6 = _____
+ 4

_____ + 4 = _____

3
⑥ 6 + 4 = _____
+④

_____ + 3 = _____

3.
⑦
③ 7 + 3 = _____
+ 4

_____ + 4 = _____

7
③ 3 + 4 = _____
+④

_____ + 7 = _____

Name _____

Make a Table

Jan is making groups of flowers. The flowers are red, blue, and yellow. Each group has 3 flowers on it. How many different groups can Jan make?

Read and Understand

You need to find how many different ways you can put the flowers together.

Plan and Solve

You can make a table.

Count how many ways you made.

There are _____ ways.

Look Back and Check

Did you find all the ways? How can you check?

Red Flowers	Blue Flowers	Yellow Flowers
3	0	0
0	3	0
0	0	3
2	1	0
2	0	1

You can have 3 flowers of one color.

You can have 2 flowers of one color and 1 flower of another color.

You can have 1 flower of each color.

Name _____

Using Related Facts

R 11-8

These two facts are related.

The addition sentence and the subtraction sentence have the same 3 numbers.

$9 + 3 = 12$

$12 - 3 = 9$

The sum of the addition sentence is the first number in the subtraction sentence.

Add. Then write a related subtraction fact.

1.

$8 + 4 = \underline{12}$

$\underline{12} - \underline{4} = \underline{8}$

2.

$7 + \underline{6} = \underline{13}$

$\underline{13} - \underline{6} = \underline{}$

3.

$9 + 2 = \underline{}$

$\underline{} - 9 = \underline{}$

4.

$8 + 5 = \underline{}$

$\underline{} - 8 = \underline{}$

5.

$9 + 7 = \underline{}$

$\underline{} - 9 = \underline{}$

6.

$8 + 7 = \underline{}$

$\underline{} - 8 = \underline{}$

© Pearson Education, Inc. 1

140 Use with Lesson 11-8.

Fact Families

This is a fact family.

$8 + 4 = 12$

$4 + 8 = 12$

Each number sentence has the same 3 numbers.

$12 - 8 = 4$

$12 - 4 = 8$

Complete each fact family. Use counters to help you.

1. | 6 | 11 | 5 |

$6 + 5 = \underline{11}$

$5 + \underline{6} = 11$

$11 - 5 = \underline{6}$

$11 - \underline{6} = 5$

2. | 9 | 5 | 14 |

$9 + 5 = \underline{}$

$5 + \underline{} = 14$

$14 - 5 = \underline{}$

$14 - \underline{} = 5$

3. | 7 | 6 | 13 |

$7 + 6 = \underline{}$

$6 + \underline{} = 13$

$13 - 6 = \underline{}$

$13 - \underline{} = 6$

Name _____

Using Addition to Subtract

$6 + 5 = 11$ $11 - 5 = \underline{6}$

> You can use an addition fact to help you write a subtraction fact with the same numbers.

Add. Then use the addition fact to help you subtract.
Use cubes if you like.

1. $4 + 9 = \underline{13}$

$13 - 9 = \underline{4}$

2. $8 + 7 = \underline{}$

$15 - 7 = \underline{}$

3. $7 + 4 = \underline{}$

$11 - 4 = \underline{}$

4. $6 + 7 = \underline{}$

$13 - 7 = \underline{}$

© Pearson Education, Inc. 1

Use with Lesson 11-10.

Name _____

Using 10 to Subtract

Subtract 13 − 7.

	Cross out 7.	What is left?	

```
  13                        3         13
 − 7                      + 3        − 7
 ____                     ____       ____
                            6          6
```

Cross out to subtract. Use counters if you like.

1.
```
   11                      2          11
  − 8                    + ⋮         − 8
  ____                   ____        ____
```

```
   3
```

2.
```
   17                      1          17
  − 9                    + □         − 9
  ____                   ____        ____
```

3.
```
   15                     □           15
  − 7                    + □         − 7
  ____                   ____        ____
```

4.
```
   16                     □           16
  − 8                    + □         − 8
  ____                   ____        ____
```

Name _____

Applying Subtraction Fact Strategies

$\begin{array}{r} 14 \\ -\ 9 \\ \hline \end{array}$ I know that $9 + 5 = 14$.
I can use the related
fact to find $14 - 9$.

$\begin{array}{r} 9 \\ +\ 5 \\ \hline 14 \end{array}$ ○○○○○○○○
○○○○○

$\begin{array}{r} 14 \\ -\ 9 \\ \hline 5 \end{array}$ ⊠⊠⊠⊠⊠⊠⊠⊠⊠○○○○○

$$10 - 9 = 1 \qquad\qquad 1 + 4 = 5$$

$\begin{array}{r} 14 \\ -\ 9 \\ \hline \end{array}$ I can use 10
to subtract.

$\begin{array}{r} 14 \\ -\ 9 \\ \hline 5 \end{array}$

Subtract.

Then circle the strategy you used.

I. $\begin{array}{r} 13 \\ -\ 7 \\ \hline 6 \end{array}$ $\boxed{7 + 6 = 13}$ use a related fact

$\begin{array}{l} 10 - 7 = 3 \\ 3 + 3 = 6 \end{array}$ use 10

2. $\begin{array}{r} 14 \\ -\ 6 \\ \hline \end{array}$ use a related fact use 10	**3.** $\begin{array}{r} 12 \\ -\ 5 \\ \hline \end{array}$ use a related fact use 10
4. $\begin{array}{r} 15 \\ -\ 6 \\ \hline \end{array}$ use a related fact use 10	**5.** $\begin{array}{r} 17 \\ -\ 9 \\ \hline \end{array}$ use a related fact use 10

Name _____

Multiple-Step Problems

Jill has 6 marbles. She gets 5 more.
How many marbles does she have in all?

$6 + 5 =$ __11__ marbles

Jill gives 8 marbles to Sal.
Now how many marbles
does Jill have?

> Think: I know Jill has 11 marbles
> in all. I know she gives 8 to
> Sal. I can subtract to find
> how many she has left.

$11 - 8 =$ __3__   Jill has __3__ marbles left.

Solve each problem.

1. Jack has 4 model cars. He gets 3 more model cars.
   How many model cars does Jack have in all?

   __3__ + __4__ = __7__ model cars

   For his birthday Jack gets 5 model cars.
   How many model cars does he have now?

   _____ + _____ = _____ model cars

2. Nicky has 6 charms on her bracelet. She buys 8 more.
   How many charms does Nicky have in all?

   _____ + _____ = _____ charms

   On the way home 4 charms are lost.
   How many charms does Nicky have now?

   _____ − _____ = _____ charms

Name _____

On the Farm

There are 12 hens in a barnyard.

4 hens are brown. The rest are white.

How many hens are white?

12 − 4 = __8__

Use a related addition fact to check your answer.

4 + 8 = __12__   So, 12 − 4 = __8__.

---

1. 4 cows are in the barn.   4
   7 cows are in the pen.   7
   3 cows are in the meadow.   + 3
   How many cows are there in all?   _____ cows

---

2. The farmer has 17 baskets   Check
   of strawberries.   17
   He sells 9 baskets.   − 9   + ___
   How many baskets are left?   17   _____ baskets

Writing in Math

3. Draw a picture of 14 eggs. Write a
   subtraction story about your picture.
   Then write a number sentence.

   _____

   _____

   _____ − _____ = _____

Adding Groups of 10

You can use what you know about adding ones
to add groups of ten.

2 ones and 5 ones are 7 ones.   2 tens and 5 tens are 7 tens.

   2   +   5   =   7   20   +   50   =   70

Write each number sentence.

1.

$$3 + 2 = 5$$ $$30 + 20 = 50$$

2.

___ + ___ = 6   ___ + ___ = 60

3.

___ + ___ = ___   ___ + ___ = ___

4.

___ + ___ = ___

5.

___ + ___ = ___

Adding Tens to Two-Digit Numbers

You can count on by tens to add.

3 tens

28 + 30   is   28 + 3 tens

28, __38__ , __48__ , __58__

28 + 30 = 58

Solve each number sentence.

1.

31, __41__ , __51__ , __61__ , __71__ , __81__

31 + 50   is   31 + __5__ tens

31 + 50 = __81__

2.

52 + 20   is   52 + _____ tens   52, _____ , _____

52 + 20 = _____

3.

33 + 40 is 33 + _____ tens   33, ____ , ____ , ____ , ____

33 + 40 = _____

Name _____

Adding Two-Digit Numbers

Find the sum of 25 and 13.

Add the ones.

Add the tens.

$5 + 3 = \underline{8}$

$2 + 1 = \underline{3}$

$25 + 13 = \underline{38}$

$20 + 10 = \underline{30}$

Draw and add the ones and tens. Find each sum.

1. Find the sum of 43 and 24.

Add the ones.

Tens	Ones
+	

Tens	Ones
+	

Add the tens.

Tens	Ones
+	

_____ + _____ = _____

_____ + _____ = _____

$43 + 24 = \underline{\hspace{1cm}}$

_____ + _____ = _____

Regrouping in Addition

Add 26 and 5.

Show 26.　　　　Add 5.

Regroup 10 ones as 1 ten.

Tens	Ones

Tens	Ones

Tens	Ones

Tens	Ones

$26 + 5 = $ **31**

Find the sum.

1. Add 16 and 7.

Show 16.　　Add 7.　　Regroup.　　Find the sum.

Tens	Ones

Tens	Ones

Tens	Ones

Tens	Ones

$16 + 7 = $ **23**

---

2. Add 28 and 5.

Show 28.　　Add 5.　　Regroup.　　Find the sum.

Tens	Ones

Tens	Ones

Tens	Ones

Tens	Ones

$28 + 5 = $ _____

© Pearson Education, Inc. 1

150　Use with Lesson 12-4.

PROBLEM-SOLVING SKILL   **R 12-5**

Exact Answer or Estimate?

Al has 2 bags of name tags.

Each bag has 12 name tags.

There are 18 children in his group.

Does he have enough name tags for all of the children?

Read and Understand

You need to know if 2 bags of name tags

are enough for 18 children.

Do you need an exact answer or an estimate?

Plan and Solve

12 is more than 10, so 12 + 12 is greater than 10 + 10.

18 is less than 10 + 10. You can estimate that there are enough.

exact answer   (estimate)

Look Back and Check

Does your answer make sense?

Is an exact answer or an estimate needed
to solve each problem?

Circle **exact answer** or **estimate.**

1. Jody wants to buy 4 stickers. They cost 7¢ each. Jody has 45¢. Does she have enough money?

    exact answer   estimate

2. Jody has 12 stickers. She has 3 pages left in her sticker book. Can she put 4 stickers on each page?

    exact answer   estimate

Subtracting Groups of 10

Subtracting groups of 10 is like subtracting ones.

$6 - 2 = \underline{4}$

$60 - 20 = \underline{40}$

Complete each number sentence.

1.

$5 - 1 = \underline{4}$ $50 - 10 = \underline{40}$

2.

$6 - 3 = \underline{\quad}$ $60 - 30 = \underline{\quad}$

3.

$7 - 4 = \underline{\quad}$ $70 - 40 = \underline{\quad}$

4.

$5 - 4 = \underline{\quad}$ $50 - 40 = \underline{\quad}$

Problem Solving *Mental Math*

Solve.

5. A star sticker and a sun sticker cost 50¢ altogether. The star sticker costs 20¢ by itself. How much does the sun sticker cost?

_____ ¢

Name _____

Subtracting Tens from Two-Digit Numbers

You can count back by tens to subtract.

43 − 20   is   43 − 2 tens   43 − 20 = __23__

Solve each number sentence.

1.

34 − 10   is   34 − __1__ ten   34 − 10 = 24

2.

52 − 30   is   52 − ____ tens   52 − 30 = ____

3.

64, ____, ____, ____, ____

64 − 40   is   64 − ____ tens   64 − 40 = ____

Name _____

Subtracting Two-Digit Numbers

Find the difference for 38 − 16.

Subtract the ones.

Subtract the tens.

Tens	Ones
3	8
− 1	6
	2

Tens	Ones
3	8
− 1	6
2	2

Write each difference.

1.

Subtract the ones.

Subtract the tens.

Tens	Ones
4	6
− 3	2

Tens	Ones
4	6
− 3	2

2.

Subtract the ones.

Subtract the tens.

Tens	Ones
5	8
− 2	5

Tens	Ones
5	8
− 2	5

© Pearson Education, Inc. 1

Name _____

Regrouping In Subtraction

Find the difference for the problem 32 − 6.

| Show 32. | Regroup 1 ten as 10 ones. | Subtract. |

Tens	Ones

Subtract 6.

Tens	Ones

Tens	Ones

$$32 - 6 = \underline{26}$$

---

1. Find the difference for the problem 46 − 8.

| Show 46. | Regroup. | Subtract. |

Tens	Ones

Subtract 8.

Tens	Ones

Tens	Ones

$$46 - 8 = \underline{38}$$

---

2. Find the difference for the problem 23 − 7.

| Show 23. | Regroup. | Subtract. |

Tens	Ones

Subtract 7.

Tens	Ones

Tens	Ones

$$23 - 7 = \underline{}$$

Name _____

Make a Graph

The bead store sells red, white, and blue beads. Which color bead did they sell the most?

> Count by tens. Then count on by fives.

Beads Sold				
	Week 1	Week 2	Week 3	Week 4
Red Beads	10	5	10	10
Blue Beads	10	5	5	10
White Beads	10	10	10	10

Read and Understand

The chart shows how many of each color beads were sold. We want to find which color sold the most.

Plan and Solve

Use the information in the chart to make a graph.
Color one box for every 5 beads sold.

> Count the boxes by fives.

Beads Sold

Red Beads										
Blue Beads										
White Beads										

0 5 10 15 20 25 30 35 40 45 50
Number of Beads Sold

The _____ beads sold the most.

Look Back and Check

How can you be sure your answer is correct?

PROBLEM-SOLVING APPLICATIONS   R 12-11
Caring for Kittens

The Kitty-Cat Pet Shop has 23 squeaky cat toys.
The store owner buys 20 more squeaky cat toys.
How many squeaky cat toys does the pet shop
have altogether?

23 and $\underline{20}$ more is how many altogether?

Use counting on by ten to add: $23 + \underline{20} = \underline{43}$

The pet shop has $\underline{43}$ squeaky cat toys.

---

1. On Monday, the Kitty-Cat Pet Shop
   sold 10 squeaky cat toys. How many
   squeaky cat toys does the store have left?

   _____ ⃝ _____ = _____ squeaky cat toys

2. Jimmy bought 5 white rubber mice
   and 4 blue rubber mice. How many
   rubber mice did he buy?

   _____ ⃝ _____ = _____ rubber mice

3. Jimmy lost 2 rubber mice. How many
   rubber mice does he have left?

   _____ ⃝ _____ = _____ rubber mice